COURTNEY CAROLA

# the weight of grief

Copyright © 2025 by Courtney Carola
Book Cover created in Canva
Featured artwork created in Canva

All rights reserved.

ISBN: 979-8-218-70230-4

## PRAISE FOR COURTNEY CAROLA

"Have Some Pride is a beautiful and accessible collection of poetry that you will not be able to put down."
- It Gets Better
for *Have Some Pride*

"Skeleton is a moving, real, and raw collection about body image. Carola doesn't sugarcoat the reality of an eating disorder, but nevertheless, her poems will give you hope and love."
- Shelby Leigh. author of Changing with the Tides
for *skeleton*

"Skeleton reads like a full body x-ray: utterly raw and starkly transparent. Honest, heartbreaking, and deeply personal, Carola's words read more like a diary than a work of poetry. If you have ever dealt with an eating disorder or struggled to love your body, this book will help you see through to yourself in new ways."
- Michelle Awad, author of Soul Trash, Space Garbage
for *skeleton*

### EARLY PRAISE FOR
### "THE WEIGHT OF GRIEF"

"In *the weight of grief,* Carola takes us on a poetic journey of the pain that comes with losing someone we love. The poems are raw, emotional and personal, but anyone who has ever experienced grief will see themselves, and their loss, in this book. Carola's poems will gently hold your hand through the grief and remind you that you're not alone."
- Shelby Leigh, bestselling author of *from sand to stars*

"Beautiful and powerful -- I read this book in one sitting. Carola took pain and turned it into poetry. The words flow beautifully, while also capturing the depths of loss and the journey grief takes us on. Anyone who has lost someone near and dear to them will relate with this book. I love poetry and was impressed with the way Carola writes, but you don't have to love poetry to be encouraged by and find solidarity in this book." - Victoria Grace Gehman, author of *Words For Weary Wanderers*

"The Weight of Griet by Courtney Carola is not a book you read, it's one you feel. I feel all of my books but this book? [cont. on next page]

## EARLY PRAISE FOR
## "THE WEIGHT OF GRIEF"

[cont. from prev page] It's a book that will stay with me all of my days. I haven't felt this way about a book in a very long time. It's a book the author poured every feeling into and it shows. If you're struggling with feelings of grief I highly recommend this book." - Amber, ARC Reader

"If I could give this book 6 stars I would [...] These poems made me feel like I was on Court and Courtney's journey in parallel, without even knowing, looking through a mirror as we both navigated our loss separately, but somehow together." - Lo, ARC Reader

"as a big fan of prose and poetry, this book is just a treasure trove of amazing words. in so little or so many words, i couldn't help but get emotional reading every poem, as one who has experienced losing someone close to me. [...] this book is a perfect representation of grief and loss that i think all of us can relate to." - Angeni, ARC Reader

# OTHER TITLES BY COURTNEY CAROLA

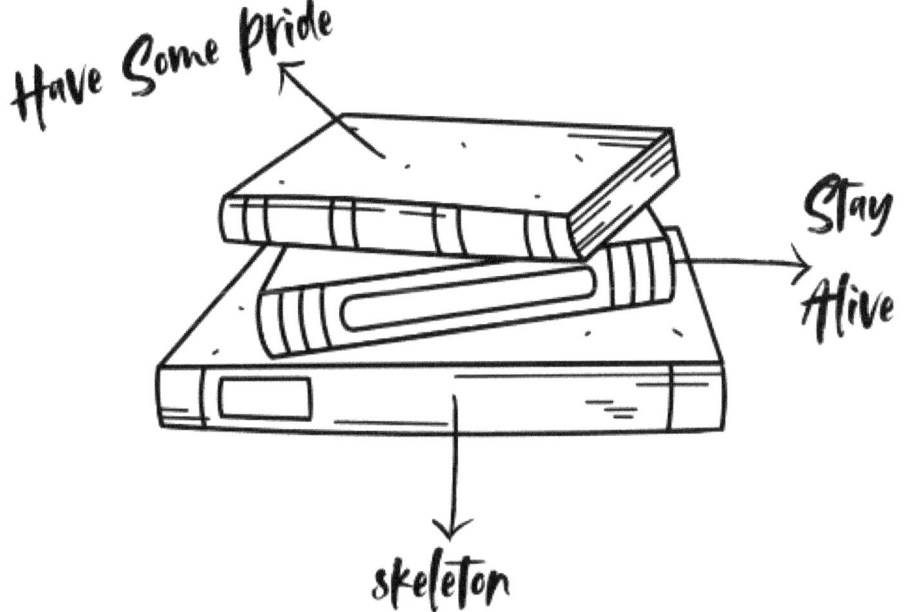

# the weight of grief

COURTNEY CAROLA

edited by Shelby Leigh

## A Note From The Author (I)

Whether your grief is a fresh wound, a scab you can't stop picking at, or an omnipresent scar, this book is for anyone in any stage of their loss. That being said, this book may bring up painful memories of your loss so please take this reminder to exercise self care before, during and after reading. For resources, see the end of the book.

Much love,
cc

written in memory of

*Courtney Marella Hendrix*

january 24, 1992 - june 18, 2023

      court,
here's everything you got to read
and everything i wish you could.

for sarah hardison

"for better or worse, but never for granted."

*If only my grief could be weighed*

*and placed with my calamity on the scales.*

*For then it would outweigh the sand of the seas—*

*no wonder my words have been rash.*

- Job 6:2-3

**PART 1**

# with you

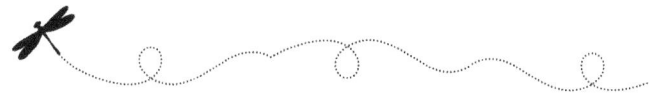

had i not met you
i would never have known
the kind of
warmth
love
support
tenderness
and friendship
that i have always dreamed of

had i not met you
i may not have realized
that dreams can come true

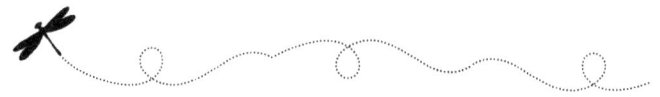

you are
the sunshine
that breaks through
my gray sky
the warmth
that reminds me
what it means to come home
you are
everything
that lights
my soul aflame
you are
everything
that makes living
a little bit brighter
a little bit nicer
a little bit easier

inside of you burns a bright
and beautiful fire
and in case you've forgotten,
your anxiety is a liar

you are loved and important
and special and rare
there are so many people
who love you, who care

you're perfect as you are
your flaws don't mean you're flawed
you may not believe,
but soon you'll see, i swear to God

your value is inherent
your existence is apparent
and without you,
this world would start to spin errant

and i know some days,
you don't know what to do
i know you're tired,
but there's so much fight left in you

i know it's been a struggle
i know you're trying hard
one day it'll be worth it
and your heart won't feel so scarred

your mind won't be a prison
one day it'll set you free
soon enough, you'll get to be
who you're meant to be

give it time and you'll see—
the dust will settle, the sun will set
i'm not a gambling man,
but for you i'd take the bet

because i love you and you matter
and please hear me when i say
i promise you, my angel,
it's all going to be okay

## HER MOTTO: A HAIKU

    atoms and purpose
    at the base of our being
    you (and i) matter

 **court**
@courtkindasunny

you matter and i matter and we matter and he matters and she matters and they matter and it a matters

our efforts to make the world better MATTER

and heckity frickin frack to anybody who says otherwise

 **court**
@courtkindasunny

but also, speak up! this is a big "you tell 'em, baby" to everyone reading this

your voice is important

you matter

 **court**
@courtkindasunny

goodnight, friendos! sometimes, you've just gotta give yourself an early night and some gentle self-care. grab your blanket and your book, say "i love you" to yourself, and call it a night if you need to. 🩶

you matter. 🤍🩶

 **court**
@courtkindasunny

in case no one has told you today:

- you are valid
- you matter

 **court**
@courtkindasunny

can i please just kiss you all on the forehead and tell you that you matter?

 **court**
@courtkindasunny

in case you need to hear it:

- you are loved.
- you matter.

 **court**
@courtkindasunny

*through gritted teeth* YOU *grunts of effort* MATTER

 **court**
@courtkindasunny

i love you. forever. you're valid, you matter, and the world is better with you here.

 **court**
@courtkindasunny

QUICK! hug yourself and tell yourself that i love you and you matter! repeat as needed!! 🤍🩶

 **court**
@courtkindasunny

goodnight, my loves. we made it.

you matter.

🤍🩶

 **court**
@courtkindasunny

your life, your feelings, your identity, and your presence in this life matter. you matter. 🩶

 **court**
@courtkindasunny

you matter, and your well-being matters. you can reschedule plans, but you never get another self

 **court**
@courtkindasunny

27. you matter. we all matter. there is no one who exists who doesn't matter.

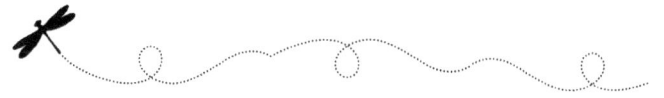

    she's known of death for so long
    knew its name before she even knew her own
    and she knows that death is the tall, dark
stranger her mother's always warned her about
    but she isn't afraid
    she never has been
    no, she calls death a bitch
    when she finds it lurking outside of the bar and
    dares it to meet her in the alley
    where she can show it who is the stronger of
the two
    but death never comes when it's expected to
    death always comes like the first snowfall of the
season;
    its arrival sudden, unexpected
    and cold

they don't understand

    like the moon, they have only seen you in fractions, only seen a sliver of who you are, a snippet of the truth. while the moon goes through phases to reveal her full self, her true self, they will not let you do the same. it is as if they have taken a picture of what they want to see, and to them, that's all there is. no more, no less. but they are wrong. there is so much more to you than meets the eye. like the moon, you are growing and changing and turning and evolving every day. like the moon, you are vast and mysterious. like the moon, you are beautiful. they don't understand now but one day they will. one day, they will see there is more of you than they have chosen to see and they will marvel in all that you have to offer. one day, they will understand.

you don't understand

    like a bear in the wintertime, the pain has hibernated under your skin, in your bones, your chest, your heart, your lungs, your head. but every day is the first day of winter and that slumber has just begun. sometimes it is as though spring will never come, the bear will never wake up, the pain will never go away. but one day, this pain may teach you something you never expected to learn. one day, you will understand.

i don't understand

    like the stars in the night sky, i have only ever seen you in moments, in hours, in instances, in certain circumstances. but what i have seen makes me believe that you are destined for greatness, that you have a fate not even you can comprehend, that you are bigger than what is and who is hurting you. from what i have seen, i believe that it will turn out fine for you. i may not understand, but i know that one day, it will all turn out fine.

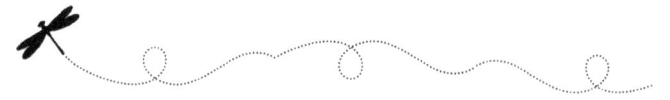

## THE FACT THAT YOU ARE ALIVE IS A MIRACLE
(after Lin Manuel Miranda)

>i don't know if it's because
>the fates said it to be
>divine interventions
>or just pure, dumb luck
>but i do know
>that you are alive
>and every day you are
>is another day of screaming "fuck you"
>to everything that tried to stop you from being
>and everyone who never believed you could be
>and i hope you scream it loud and proud
>because you're here now

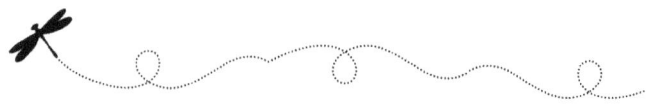

the odds might have been stacked against you
but you have time on your side
the years you've already survived
spread out behind you like a superhero's cape
and are held up by the winds of tomorrow
let the world watch you fly
and stay alive
for you to live
is more than enough

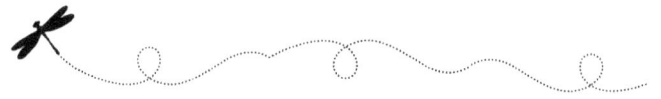

to my little bird with your wings aflame
i know lately you don't feel like brilliance
like you are only what you've just became
a mound of ash, no hope of resilience

but i swear to you, the sky is in sight
earthy ground is not all that you will see
and again you will rise; you will take flight
what you are now is not all you can be

and i know you feel like you've been left behind
but i swear, i will stay here by your side
even when the world treats you so unkind
even when you soar away, satisfied

to my little bird with your wings ablaze
remember me as you near the sun's rays

PART 2

# without you

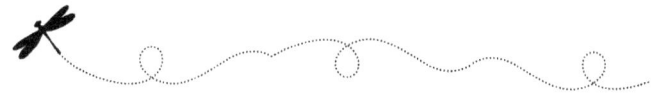

BEAST (i)

grief is a beast
and i am the neck
it sunk its teeth into
jaw locked around me with such vigor
one might have mistaken it for a lover
the beast didn't drain my blood
or steal the life from my eyes
but rather
trapped me
i didn't get the luxury of a castle
just the maw of a monster
hellbent on keeping me caught up
in an inescapable embrace
though i wished the beast would have simply
killed me
it didn't
it wouldn't
instead i was left used and discarded
and there was the beast, ready to move on to
the next victim

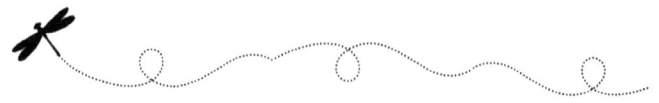

in its aftermath, i lay there
body unmoving, eyes wide open
with no choice but to watch the beast
as it tore through
what was once a peaceful village
our town became nothing more than
carnage
the damage no one could undo
though the townsfolk raised their
pitchforks and held fire in angry hands
there was no running grief out of town

my best friend died in june
and it rained for days after
as if the sky itself was mourning
a loss so great
it couldn't contain its own grief
a grief, i'm sure, not unlike my own
for i, too, am a rain cloud
constantly pouring myself empty
at the thought of a life lived
while she's lost her's

it's mid-july
and though i squint my eyes
every time i step outside
i am still waiting for the clouds to part
and the dark shadows to fade
into something similar, like light
perhaps a misty haze took over my vision
the first time i blinked
and opened my eyes to a world
without her in it
how else could you explain a fog
so thick in the middle of summer?

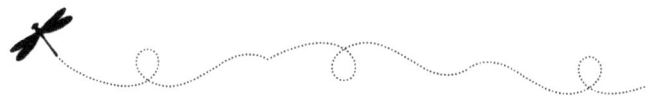

august's heat
melts into september's breeze
sending october's leaves swirling
the fall bringing the rise of november
until the chill of december
blows in
but no matter the season
it still feels like that day in june

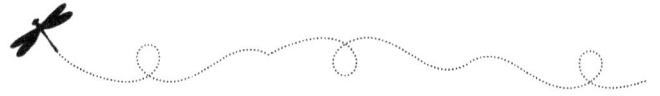

i've never missed anyone the way i miss you

this is not to say i've never loved and lost before
but losing you felt like a rug being pulled out
from under me
i didn't even realize
it had been yanked until i fell
and crashed

plunged into the earth
that stole you from me

i was bruised
and you were buried
and fuck, this isn't how it's supposed to be

this wasn't how it's supposed to be

i've never missed anyone the way i miss you
and i miss you in a way that never leaves me

on the first day you left us
the loss wrapped its arms around me
and hasn't let go
loosened its grip, maybe
but still got me

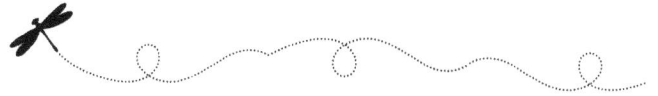

your mom told me
you've gone home to be with the Lord
but i can't understand what she means because
your home is here

it's always been here
on earth, with us
with me

and who am i
to argue with what her faith says but
i've got to say,
it isn't fair

hey God,
i know she was yours first
but i needed her more

(and i still do)

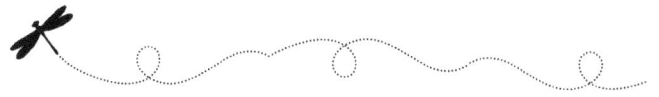

the day you died, i woke up in utter darkness

it was then i learned
that grief
is an endless midnight
and i fear my eyes will never
adjust

you see,
i was pushed into the belly of the beast
it swallowed me whole and in its stomach, i was
lost
in a lack of light
the days bled into one another until
yesterday and tomorrow
became barely discernible
and i am still lost in the pit of grief
unsure how to start a fire to freedom
or pray my way out
all i can do is wait
for my eyes to adjust

THIS IS THE PART OF DYING THAT THE MOVIES NEVER GET RIGHT:

>the director says "action!"
>and the main character gets the news
>in a pretty way
>awoken gently in the middle of the night
>a phone call with care
>a doctor's kind face
>the news is muted by a swell of sad music
>tears are silent
>hugs are given—

>>but in real life
>>your best friend is a thousand miles
>>away when she dies
>>and you'll find out a day later
>>there's no music, only the ringing in
>>your ears
>>as you try to process what you just read
>>on facebook

(there was no one to hold you in their
arms as the news was broken to you)
there was nothing pretty about it
there is nothing pretty about death in
real life

then the director shouts "cut!"
and everyone goes back to their lives
there's no hesitation to continue living

    and in real life, there's no hesitation
    either
    because real life doesn't care that you're
    grieving
    your bills
    your job
    your groceries
    your dirty laundry
    and even dirtier dishes

they all still demand your time
your attention
your energy that you no longer have
because it's all being spent trying to
keep up with a world
that won't stop spinning
though you desperately need it to pause

you wait for the director
to pause the scene
but they never do

## I HAVE TO BELIEVE THIS ROCKY ROAD THAT I TAKE WILL BRING ME TO YOU
(after CMH)

and what's a rockier road
than going through life after you've lost yours?
now, when i walk,
i feel your company
in the breeze of the wind
or
in the silent fall of the rain
or
in the warm kiss of the sun
ultimately
i am still traveling alone
and no ground has ever felt
so unsteady
my destination has never been
so unclear

PATREON POST-IT (3.11.1...

I have to believe this rocky road that I take will bring me to you

♥ CMH

and everyday, i ask myself,
"just where will this take me?"
knowing that the only place i want to go
is wherever you are
but you've gone somewhere i can't reach now
so far from me
and yet,
i keep on going

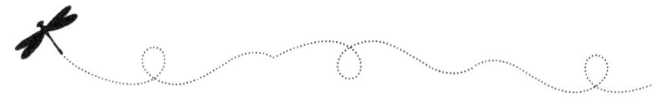

since the day you left
i have been looking high and low for you
in the shape of a cloud
(that one sort of looks like you)
or in a song on the radio
(i'll never forget how much you loved this one)
or in the glow of a rainbow
(is it a message from you?
a sign that you're still watching over me from so far away?)
i have been searching for you
everywhere
in everything
not a day goes by when i am not constantly looking for you
or maybe
i just want to know
to let myself believe
that you're still somewhere
that there's still a chance you're just out of my reach

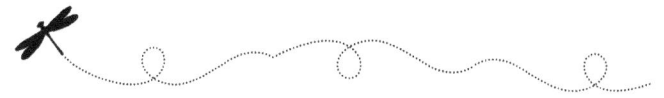

## A RECURRING DREAM

    i only ever see you at night

    when my eyes close
    yours reopen
    and you smile
    that smile i could never forget
    i hold a cup of coffee that grows cold in one hand
    while my other grips yours in a comforting embrace
    a hug i never got
    we sit across from each other like two friends catching up over dinner
    and it's so easy to forget
    that you're gone

    i never hear your voice
    but you talk to me
    your eyes shine like death never stole their light from you

blue-green ink share stories of heaven
and write me reassurances
you tell me that you're okay
and i can pretend
that i'm okay too

it's hell
waking up
then remembering

## GRIEF AS A SPIDER

>when you first entered my home
>i wanted you gone
>you, a nuisance on my life
>an uninvited guest
>trying to make a home
>where you never lived before
>i was here first
>and you had no right to sneak in
>and demand all of my attention
>i am so much bigger than you
>but you've made me feel
>so small
>i'm the one getting stepped on by you
>you, just a visitor
>not a tenant or a roommate
>you, who can come and go as you please
>so why can't you just leave?
>what brings you to my house of all places?
>after all

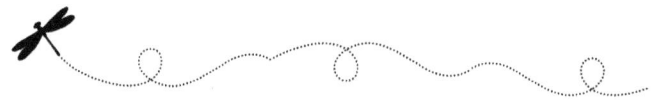

it didn't need to be my home
that you crept into in the first place
and sure
maybe
there's a reason why
it's my house you've chosen
maybe
you came to me on purpose
maybe

maybe
i should give you a chance
see what it is that brought you my way
maybe
instead of fearing you
i should give you a chance
to live by my side
maybe
i shouldn't be so hasty
in my attempts to evict you

your absence lingers like the last splash of color
as the sun sinks down on the horizon
like the beauty of dusk, you were here
and then in a moment, you were gone
and though i've tried to capture your beauty
in a photograph or two
they don't pay homage to your memory
in a way that can mirror the light
that once defined your presence

as darkness falls, slowly but surely,
and an indigo hue replaces
the vibrant color created from your smile,
i can't help but to think
you were never meant to dim
or desaturate
you were never meant to fade

if only i could turn back the clock
if only the sun could rise one more time

it feels wrong
living
while you no longer are

like spilled salt thrown over my shoulder
the stars sprinkle throughout the sky
and i turn your name into constellations
playing connect the dots with the nighttime
just to see you one more time

because now you're a piece of the night sky
i so desperately hope to find you in
a twinkle
that resembles your eyes
or a glistening glow that could rival
the brightness of your smile
i search for signs from you more often than
i find myself wishing on shooting stars
that someway
somehow
you'll come back to me

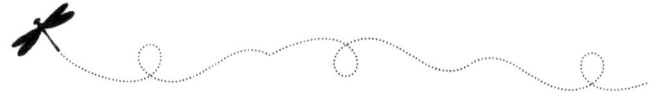

i should know better than to ask for five more
minutes because i know i will get greedy and
five will become ten then fifteen an
hour and soon i'll be asking for
one more day one more
week or month or maybe
i'll be asking to reverse
the clock
turn
the
minute
hand back
to when you
were still alive when i
didn't have to be me without
you i don't just want five more
minutes if i had it my way you'd still be here

## IMMORTAL JELLYFISH

they say our loved ones
never truly leave us
that not even death can keep us apart
because they find us again
in other forms
in constellations or songs
in butterflies or our dreams

so far
you've found me as
shapes in clouds
and a dragonfly hovering nearby

but i wish
you'd come to me
as a jellyfish

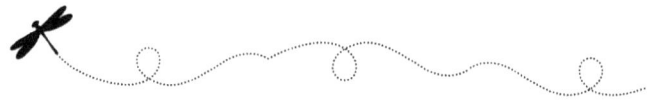

the translucent kind
red in the middle
smaller than the nail on my pinky finger
with ninety tentacles
pushing it through the ocean
swimming freely
and cheating death whenever it comes

i wish
you'd come to me
as a jellyfish
able to
at any given moment
go back to a polyp

back to you

i wish it were that simple
that your spirit could return to earth
unable to die again

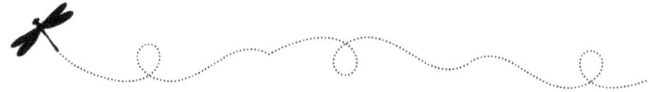

TWO TRUTHS AND A LIE

1. everything's okay, except i am so afraid of forgetting you, in big ways and small—the sound of your voice and your favorite colors and everything that made you, you. there are reminders everywhere but how long until i have to search for you instead of simply thinking of you? how long until you stop existing completely?
2. everything's okay, except i can't stop feeling sad about everything you don't get to experience anymore—songs you would've played on repeat, movies you would've loved to see. every time a new piece of media unveils itself, i find myself mourning all over again instead of just enjoying something that we both could've loved together.
3. everything's okay.

"how are you holding up?" they ask.

> not a day goes by when i don't miss her terribly / i still look for her in every cloud that floats by / i dream about her so much that when i wake up, i have to remind myself that she's gone and somehow, that hurts more than the day i found out i lost her / i still feel guilty that i'm alive and she's not / i don't understand why i'm alive when she's not / some days, i can only think about how she deserves to be alive and i don't / but i am and she's not and it isn't fair / it isn't fair / it isn't fucking fair.

"i'm okay," i reply.

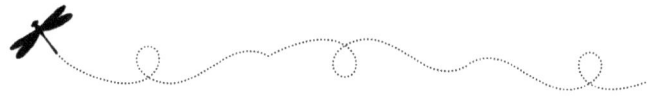

you're gone
but you're still
everywhere

in the breeze that blows
and the sun that shines
in the books i've yet to read
and shows i've yet to see

you're gone
but
you're still here
in photos and videos
and saved voicemails
and hidden notes stored for safekeeping

you're gone
but not really
no
not really

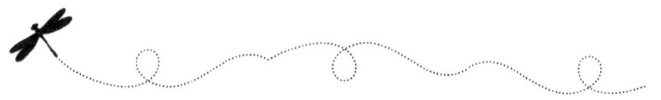

happy birthday, my angel
did the clouds rushing by
help you blow out your candles?
did the angels' choir
sing to you the way we used to?

happy birthday, my angel
there's an open seat at the table for you
i stopped at the store
and picked up a cake for you
i didn't count the candles
because i don't want to remember
that soon we'll be the same age
then i'll be older
i'll be older
and you'll always be stuck in the middle
of your last trip around the sun

happy birthday, my angel
each candle i blow out
is a wish for you
for your smile to return
for your pain to be gone
(but i hope you don't mind if
i make one for me too)

happy birthday, my angel
i wish you were still here

## YOUR GHOST AND I CATCH UP OVER PASTA
(after Amy Kay)

      i can't believe it's been a year / i brought the parmesan cheese / i'm not doing any better / but i'm trying / do you miss me as much as i miss you? / i can't stop writing about you / i feel guilty writing about anything else / or anyone else / how's your mom? / have you seen your dad? / it must be nice, getting to spend so much time with your loved ones again / does it make me a bad person that i'm jealous of them? / but this / this is nice / the garlic bread / the rotini / you / with me / i'm really glad it doesn't hurt you to enjoy this meal

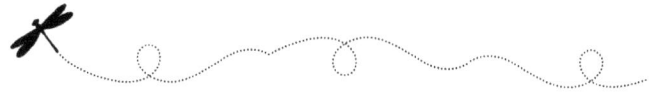

## AN INCOMPLETE LIST OF EVERYTHING YOU'VE MISSED SINCE YOU DIED

1. time feels so different now that you're gone. sometimes it moves like the tortoise—other times, the hare. which is to say that some days, i've blinked and an entire month has gone by and i realize that i'm still breathing—other days, it's the hour after i lost you and i'm trying to figure out how i'm supposed to navigate my life without you. but no matter how much time does pass, i think of you every day. i miss you every day.
2. i said the "d" word about you only once before this poem because to say your name and "died" in the same sentence feels like being on day fifteen of god's thirty day torrential downpour; at this point, it's hard to believe there's any solace in sight.

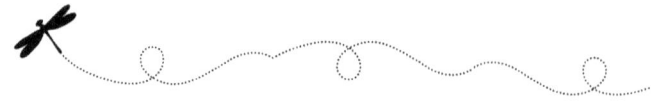

3. i saw a dragonfly outside of my job every day for three months after losing you, and it only took a week before i believed it was you—or a sign from you—or mother nature taking pity on me and just giving me something to believe in. but for three months, i had you by my side again.
4. i spent seven months falling in love, then another seven months trying to heal from it. i spent fourteen months wishing i could tell you about it.
5. i wrote seventy-two new poems that you'll never get to read, and my heart broke seventy-two times each moment i remembered that you'll never get to read them.
6. it took me five months before i was ready to get a tattoo of your favorite animal because for five months, i pretended that you were still alive.
7. our favorite book became a movie and the first time i watched it, i cried because you won't get to.
8. i saw you in twenty-two sunsets.

9. or maybe i just convinced myself twenty-two times that you were trying to reach me from heaven.
10. it took eighteen sessions before i told my therapist about you.
11. i have three hundred and forty days until my next birthday. in three hundred and forty days, i'll be older than you. i was never meant to be older than you.
12. i spent over an hour reading through almost every message you ever sent me and my only regret was not telling you "i love you" more.
13. someone else mourning asked, *at what point do you start to feel normal again*? it's been over a year and i still don't think i feel "normal" but i think i've gotten used to living around the shadows of grief so much that i'm no longer afraid of the dark.
14. i've seen seven hundred and thirty 11:11s and used every one to wish for a miracle; that you'll somehow come back home
15. me.

BEAST (ii)

sometimes
i see grief standing at the edge of town
lurking in the shadows
as it waits
for what?
for me?
for someone new?
sometimes
we lock eyes
and i remember how
the beast roared and raged
and here i am,
the remnants of its rampage:
bloodied
and bruised
but
(somehow)
still breathing

there are days
when i am able to let grief cover me
like a blanket

and on those days
i find myself taking comfort
beneath its weight
the way it encourages me
to sink down into my mattress
and simply exist as a person grieving
not someone trapped in the confines of grief

    on those days
        i am able to separate my grief from myself
        the same way i can push the covers off of my
body every morning
        and on those days
        i no longer need to float through life
        with it wrapped around my shoulders
        haunting my own life instead of living it

    on those days
    the weight of grief
    doesn't hurt to carry

*"Euphoria" season 2, episode 2*
*timestamp: 31:23*

Need help dealing with grief?
GriefShare Grief & Loss Support Groups are here for you: https://www.griefshare.org/

The Dinner Party is a platform for grieving 21-45-year-olds to find community, peer-led support, and build lasting relationships.
https://www.thedinnerparty.org/

Need to vent?
Text **HOME** to **741741** to connect with a volunteer Crisis Counselor

Grief in Common is a free website designed to connect those who are grieving based on background and similar circumstances of loss.
https://www.griefincommon.com/

Help is available
Speak with someone today
988 Suicide and Crisis Lifeline

A Note From The Author (II)

My beautiful friend Courtney was a lot of things: a daughter, a dog mom, a dedicated partner, a devout Christian, a writer, an artist, a fan of Pentatonix, Hozier, Hamilton and Wicked. She was also disabled and not ashamed to say it. Court was born with minimulticore congenital myopathy. This condition is a rare congenital myopathy characterized by the presence of minicores (small, round areas) in muscle fibers that affects approximately one in every twenty thousand people.

For Court, this condition predominantly affected her muscle tone; in her own words, "[she has] never taken an unassisted step, nor can [she] lift [her] arms or beat a child at arm wrestling." Court's circulatory, respiratory and digestive systems were also affected by this condition, as well as her being very prone to infections and her body was slow to recover from any illness or injury. Living with this condition, Court's life expectancy was fifteen.

She lived to be thirty-one.

If you think that's incredible, there's no doubt that it is. Life dealt Court the worst hand but she still played the game, and played it well. But what was even more incredible was Court herself. She, single handedly, did so much to try and raise awareness about her own condition through her art and writing. She was well aware that she was somehow a textbook case and an anomaly.

When I think of Court, I think of how she never wanted anyone to feel like an anomaly. I think of how if she were still here, she would use her voice to do just that. If I can do anything with my voice, I would like to continue to do what she strived to do: educate as many people as possible on minimulticore congenital myopathy and normalize talking about physical and mental disabilities. If I can implore you to do anything, it's to take the time out of your day to learn more about my dear friend's condition. With education comes research, with research comes awareness, and awareness will do so much - but most importantly, it will help someone feel so much less alone. And Court, with her huge heart and fierce determination, wanted nothing more than simply that.

There's so much more I could say about Court, but I think leaving you with this quote from her says more than I could ever say:

*"Life is hard and scary and painful, but it is also fun and silly and sexy, and I think it's important to see all of that."*

Court, I love you. I miss you. I hope I'm making you proud. I hope Heaven is as beautiful as you are. See you on the other side, my best pal.

## CREDITS

*THE FACT THAT YOU'RE ALIVE IS A MIRACLE* - Hamilton: An American Musical (2015), Lin-Manuel Miranda.

*I HAVE TO BELIEVE THIS ROCKY ROAD THAT I TAKE WILL BRING ME TO YOU* - Courtney Hendrix (2018)

*A RECURRING DREAM* - ESCAPRIL Day Fourteen (2024), Savannah Brown

*IMMORTAL JELLYFISH* - The Broposal (2025), Sonora Reyes

*YOUR GHOST AND I CATCH UP OVER PASTA* - FOUR FRIENDS CATCH UP OVER PASTA (2024), Amy Kay

ACKNOWLEDGEMENTS

Whenever a book goes from an idea, to a Pinterest board, to something actually written with the attempt of going somewhere, it truly takes a village to get it moving. And how lucky am I to have a village like mine.

To my amazing editor, Shelby: you are truly a wizard with words, and you have helped me (and my writing) flourish. Thank you for helping me blossom and bloom.

To my best friend, Zaneta: it took you only seconds to call me after I told you Court had passed. You were the first person I told about "the weight of grief" and you've been my sounding board ever since. Your support in all its forms means more to me than I could ever begin to express. Thank you for everything.

To my girls, Kat and Tia: your love keeps me going like no other. Thank you both for helping to heal my heart day in and day out.

To my soul sister, Devon: your genuine curiosity and care from the moment you knew I was working on this book has lifted me up in ways you'll never know. Thank you for believing in me.

To my momma: thank you for being my first ever and number one fan.

To Angeni, Mija, Ashley, Amanda, Lisa, Victoria Grace, Caitlyn, Lauren, Michaela, and Amber, my amazing ARC readers: from the moment you expressed interest in my book, I was exuberantly grateful. Thank you for your support.

And, finally, to my readers, whether a faithful or a first-timer: thank you. Thank you. Thank you.

## ABOUT THE AUTHOR

Courtney Carola is a self-published author from southern New Jersey; "the weight of grief" is her fourth collection of poetry. When she isn't writing or reading, she likes to spend her time contemplating her entire existence so she can adequately describe herself on biography sections of various websites.

## CONNECT WITH ME

 @drunk.on.writing

 @drunk.on.writing

BEFORE YOU GO...

If you enjoyed this book, even a little, please consider leaving a review on Amazon or Goodreads! Reviews help encourage new readers as well as support authors, especially indie authors like myself. Not to mention, positive reviews just make me happy and they are SO appreciated!

Much love!
xoxo, cc

www.ingramcontent.com/pod-product-compliance
Lightning Source LLC
Chambersburg PA
CBHW070620050426
42450CB00011B/3085